Printed in Great Britain
by Amazon

27390336R00064